God's little book of

Wisdom
and
Caring.

by
Wendy Bradley

First published in 2011
Copyright © 2011
Autumn House Publishing (Europe) Ltd

British Library Cataloguing in Publication Data.
A catalogue record for this book is
available from the British Library.

ISBN 978-1-906381-99-8
Published by Autumn House (Europe),
Grantham, Lincolnshire.

Designed by Abigail Murphy

Printed in Thailand

Unless otherwise indicated, Bible quotes are taken
from *The New Living Translation* (Tyndale).
Other versions used, indicated by initials:
AB = *Amplified Bible* (Zondervan)
NKJV = *New King James Version* (Thomas Nelson)

When the problems of life are getting you down, it can be hard to keep looking up. I pray this little book will bring you comfort and help you to know that when your head is perpetually down you can read about God and realise he is with you in every situation, and he is right here, right now. May God bless you, dear reader.

Hope

Having the assurance
Of the
Promise of
Eternal Life.

Mercy

Compassion or forgiveness shown
towards an enemy or offender.

Old French and Latin pity

Salvation

by grace
through faith.

(Ephesians 2:8)

Take time to read,
Take time to think,
It is the road to wisdom.
Take time to laugh,
Take time to love,
It is the road to being alive.
Take time to give,
Take time to pray,
It is the way to God.

Unknown

The bottom line?

Love people, but only trust in God.

Word for Today

Lord, I offer you this day's troubles.
Give me:
Strength to bear them,
Wisdom to handle them,
Compassion for those
who bring them;
Peace be their outcome.

Ray Simpson, Celtic Prayer

We can say with confidence, 'The Lord
is my helper, so I will not be afraid.
What can mere mortals do to me?'

Hebrews 13:6

By prevailing over all obstacles and
distractions, one may unfailingly arrive
at his chosen goal or destination.
Christopher Columbus

Duty makes us do things well, but love
makes us do them beautifully.

Phillips Brooks

Forgiveness doesn't make the other
person right; it makes you free.
Stormie Omartian

Be eager to encourage someone in his faith, but also be encouraged by others in your faith. In this way you will both be blessed.

(Roman 1:12)

Happiness is not getting what you
want; it is wanting what you get.

Unknown

Kind words like good deeds
are eternal; you never know
where their influence will end.

H. Jackson Brown

Jesus Christ is the same yesterday,
today and forever.

Hebrews 13:8

When walking through the
'valley of shadows', remember, a
shadow is cast by a Light.

H. K. Barclay

The only way to have
a friend is to be one.

Ralph Waldo Emerson

Humour is the prelude to faith, and
laughter is the beginning of prayer.

Reinhold Niebuhr

If you stay focused on yourself you
are guaranteed to be miserable.

H. Jackson Brown

Lord Jesus Christ, you are
the journey: the journey's end
and the journey's beginning.

Dean Mayne

We can't plan life.
All we can do is to be available for it.

Lauryn Hill

Those who live in the shelter of the Most High will find rest in the shadow of the Almighty.

Psalm 91:1

Peace begins with a smile.
Mother Teresa

Knowledge speaks,
but wisdom listens.
Jimi Hendrix

Always be joyful. Keep on praying.
No matter what happens, always be
thankful, for this is God's will for
you who belong to Christ Jesus.

1 Thessalonians 5:16-18

If God can work through me,
he can work through anyone.

St Francis of Assisi

Coming together is a beginning.
Keeping together is progress.
Working together is success.
Henry Ford

If you can't sleep, then get up
and do something instead of lying
there worrying. It's the worry that
gets you, not the lack of sleep.

Dale Carnegie

The world is a great mirror.
It reflects back to you what you are.
If you are loving, if you are friendly,
if you are helpful, the world will prove
loving and friendly and helpful to you.
The world is what you are.

Thomas Dreier

Believe that life is worth living, and
your belief will help you create that.

William James

Though our feelings come and go,
God's love for us does not.

C. S. Lewis

Always keep that happy attitude.
Pretend you are holding a
beautiful, fragrant bouquet.

Candice M. Pope

Give according to your means and beyond your means, of your own free will, but first give yourself to God.

(2 Corinthians 8:3, 4, 5)

Think positively and masterfully, with
confidence and faith, and life becomes
more secure, more fraught with action,
richer in achievement and experience.

Eddie Rickenbacker

I pray that God, who gives you hope,
will keep you happy and full of
peace as you believe in him.
May you overflow with hope
through the power of the Holy Spirit.

Romans 15:13

How wonderful it is that nobody
need wait a single moment before
starting to improve the world.

Anne Frank

For he will rescue you from every trap and protect you from the fatal plague. He will shield you with his wings. He will shelter you with his feathers. His faithful promises are your armour and protection.

Psalm 91:3, 4

Regardless of how little you have,
you can always give comfort
and encouragement.

H. Jackson Brown

Zeal of God, stir my frame.
Truth of God, light my way.
Peace of God, redeem my past.
Love of God, fill my being.

Ray Simpson, Celtic Prayer

Good friends are like stars. . . .
You don't always see them, but you
know they are always there.

Unknown

You can't change circumstances
and you can't change people,
but God can change you.

Evelyn A. Theissen

Be strong and courageous! Don't be afraid of the King of Assyria or his mighty army, for there is a power far greater on our side! He may have a great army, but they are just men. We have the Lord our God to help us and to fight our battles for us.

2 Chronicles 32:7, 8

We are not put on this earth for
ourselves, but are here for each other.
If you are there always for others,
then in time of need someone
will be there for you.

Jeff Warner

Wisdom is knowing what to do next;
Skill is knowing how to do it, and
Virtue is doing it.

David Starr Jordan

Without courage,
wisdom bears no fruit.
Baltazar Gracian

The one who plants and the one who waters work as a team with the same purpose. Yet they will be rewarded individually, according to their own hard work.

1 Corinthians 3:8

Aerodynamically, the bumblebee shouldn't be able to fly, but the bumblebee doesn't know that, so it goes on flying anyway.

Mary Kay Ash

He has showered his kindness
on us, along with all wisdom
and understanding.

Ephesians 1:8

Nobody has ever measured, not even
poets, how much a heart can hold.

Zelda Fitzgerald

And who of you by worrying and
being anxious can add one unit of
measure (cubit) to his stature
or to the span of his life?

Matthew 6:27, AB

It is only in sorrow bad weather
masters us; in joy we face
the storm and defy it.

Amelia Barr

God loves us the way we are,
but too much to leave us that way.

Leighton Ford

The happiness of your life depends
upon the quality of your thoughts: . . .
take care that you entertain no
notions unsuitable to virtue
and reasonable nature.

Marcus Aurelius

Thoughts lead on to purposes;
purposes go forth in action; actions
form habits; habits decide character;
and character fixes our destiny.

Tryon Edwards

A winner is someone who recognises
his God-given talents, works his tail off
to develop them into skills and uses
these skills to accomplish his goals.

Larry Bird

It is not the cares of today, but the cares of tomorrow that weigh a man down. For the needs of today we have corresponding strength given. For the morrow we are told to trust. It is not ours yet.

George MacDonald

He is so rich in kindness that he
purchased our freedom through
the blood of his Son,
and our sins are forgiven.

Ephesians 1:7

Faith doesn't demand details, it just
keeps moving obediently forward,
believing God for the right result.

Word for Today

Share each other's troubles and
problems, and in this way
obey the law of Christ.

Galatians 6:2

All that I have seen teaches me to trust
God for all I have not seen.
Unknown

No duty is more urgent than
that of returning thanks.
Unknown

The Lord is my light and my salvation
– so why should I be afraid?
The Lord protects me from danger
– so why should I tremble?

Psalm 27:1

While we are postponing,
life speeds by.
Seneca

Things will probably come out right,
but sometimes it takes strong
nerves just to watch.

Hedley Donovan

A man's heart plans his way,
but the LORD directs his steps.

Proverbs 16:9, NKJV

Trust the past to God's mercy, the
present to God's love and the
future to God's providence.

St Augustine

A keen sense of humour helps us
overlook the unbecoming,
understand the unconventional,
tolerate the unpleasant,
overcome the unexpected and
outlast the unbearable.

Billy Graham

I command you – be strong and
courageous! Do not be afraid or
discouraged. For the LORD your God
is with you wherever you go.

Joshua 1:9

May you live every day of your life.

Jonathan Swift

Love each other with genuine affection, and take delight in honouring each other.

Romans 12:10

If you want others to be happy,
practise compassion.
If you want to be happy,
practise compassion.

The Dalai Lama

Love life and life will love you back.
Love people and they will
love you back.

Arthur Rubinstein

I believe in the sun
when it is not shining,
I believe in love even
when I cannot feel it,
I believe in God,
even when he is silent.

Jewish prisoner

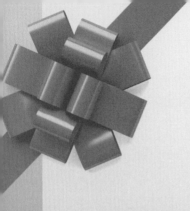

Meeting interesting people
depends less on where you
go than who you are.
Lasting Friendship

Adapt yourself to the things
among which your lot has been
cast and love sincerely the fellow
creatures with whom destiny has
ordained that you should live.

Marcus Aurelius

We may let go all things which we cannot carry into the eternal life.

Anna R. Brown Lindsey

Surround yourself with the best
people you can find, delegate
authority, and don't interfere as
long as the policy you've decided
upon is being carried out.

Ronald Reagan

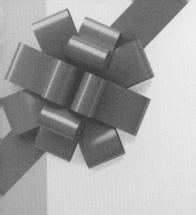

Enjoy your own life without
comparing it with that of another.

Marquis de Condorcet

Not life, but good life,
is to be chiefly valued.

Socrates

Let me teach you, because I am
humble and gentle, and you
will find rest for your souls.

Matthew 11:29

Your attitude should be the same
that Christ Jesus had. Though
he was God, . . . he made
himself nothing; he took the
humble position of a slave.

Philippians 2:5, 6, 7

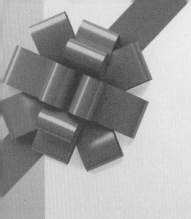

The quickest way to get what you want
is to help others get what they want.

Lasting Friendship

It is by forgiving that one is forgiven.

Mother Teresa

The true measure of a man is how
he treats someone who can do
him absolutely no good.

Samuel Johnson

Never forget the three powerful
resources you always have available
to you: love, prayer and forgiveness.

H. Jackson Brown

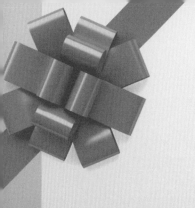

Love is not blind – it sees more,
not less. But because it sees
more, it is willing to see less.

Julius Gordon

The LORD protects those of childlike faith; I was facing death, and then he saved me. Now I can rest again, for the LORD has been so good to me.

Psalm 116:6, 7

The unthankful heart . . .
discovers no mercies;
but the thankful heart . . .
will find, in every hour,
some heavenly blessings.

Henry Ward Beecher

Well done is better than well said.

Benjamin Franklin

Faith is to believe what we do not see;
and the reward of this faith is
to see what we believe.

St Augustine

Let the thirsty ones come – anyone
who wants to. Let them come and
drink the water of life without charge.

Revelation 22:17

Sometimes it is not enough to do our best; we must do what is required.

Winston Churchill

The smile is the lighting system
of the face and the heating
system of the heart.

Unknown

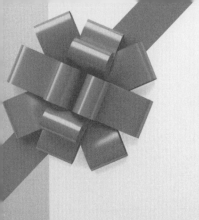

Always do right – this will gratify
some and astonish the rest.

Mark Twain

When the Holy Spirit controls our lives, he will produce this kind of fruit in us: love, joy, peace, patience, kindness, goodness, faithfulness, gentleness and self-control.

Galatians 5:22, 23

You have heard me teach many things that have been confirmed by many reliable witnesses. Teach these great truths to trustworthy people who are able to pass them on to others.

2 Timothy 2:2

Trust first in those who say,
'I made a mistake.'
Lasting Friendship

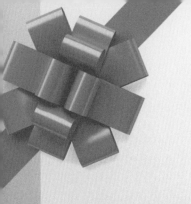

Criticism, like rain, should be gentle
enough to nourish a man's growth
without destroying his roots.

Frank A. Clark

O God, give me [us] the strength
to look up and not down,
to look forward and not back,
to look out and not in, and
to lend a hand.

Edward Everett Hale

Please, LORD, rescue me!
Come quickly, LORD, and help me. . . .
I am poor and needy, but the Lord is
thinking about me right now.
You are my helper and Saviour.
Do not delay, O my God!

Psalm 40:13, 17

Whatever you need, God has it.
Whatever you give up,
he will repay many times over.
Whatever you're willing to walk away
from ultimately determines what he
can trust you with.

Word for Today

Help me to run straight,
To go all out,
And to give my best.

Ray Simpson

Opportunities multiply
as they are seized.
Sun Tzu

Some cause happiness wherever they
go; others, whenever they go!
Oscar Wilde

He lets me rest in green meadows;
he leads me beside peaceful streams.
He renews my strength.
He guides me along right paths,
bringing honour to his name.

Psalm 23:2, 3

He that would live in
peace and at ease,
Must not speak all he knows,
or judge all he sees.
Benjamin Franklin

If you don't feel like being pleasant,
courteous and kind, act that way
and the feelings will come.

H. Jackson Brown

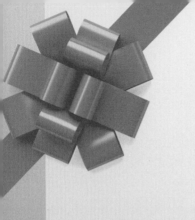

People living deeply
have no fear of death.

Anaïs Nin

God never promised an easy ride.
He does promise a safe arrival.
Unknown

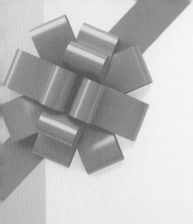

A good heart is better than
all the heads in the world.

Edward Bulwer-Lytton

God is my shield, saving those
whose hearts are true and right.

Psalm 7:10

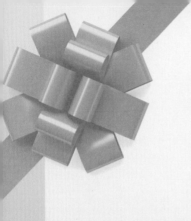

Hospitality consists in a little fire,
a little food, and an immense quiet.

Ralph Waldo Emerson

Do not be afraid,
for I have ransomed you.
I have called you by name;
you are mine.

Isaiah 43:1

Four things,
which are not in Thy treasury,
I lay before Thee, Lord,
with this petition:
My nothingness, my wants,
My sins, and my contrition.

Robert Southey

The best way to cheer yourself up is to
try to cheer somebody else up.

Mark Twain

Do what you're good at and
everything else will fall into place.
Willnett Crockett

Your love for one another will prove to
the world that you are my disciples.

John 13:35

Goodness of friendship
grow between us:
friendship with insight,
friendship with faithfulness,
friendship with the light touch.

Ray Simpson, Celtic Prayers

In a full heart there is room for
everything, and in an empty
heart there is room for nothing.

Antonio Porchia

Don't be afraid to give your best to what seemingly are small jobs. Every time you conquer one it makes you that much stronger. If you do the little jobs well, the big ones will tend to take care of themselves.

Dale Carnegie

He who sows courtesy reaps
friendship; he who plants
kindness gathers love.

Saint Basil

Act as if what you do
makes a difference.
It does.
William James

Don't let what you cannot do
interfere with what you can do.

John Wooden

Don't worry about anything;
instead, pray about everything.
Tell God what you need, and thank
him for all he has done. If you do this,
you will experience God's peace,
which is far more wonderful than the
human mind can understand. His
peace will guard your hearts and
minds as you live in Christ Jesus.

Philippians 4:6, 7